Weave, coil & plait
CRAFTY CONTAINERS
from recycled materials

This book is dedicated to my parents, Ken and Irene Walpole, who have always unfailingly encouraged and supported my need to make things.

Weave, coil & plait
CRAFTY CONTAINERS
from recycled materials

LOIS WALPOLE

SEARCH PRESS

First published in Great Britain 1997

Search Press Limited
Wellwood, North Farm Road,
Tunbridge Wells, Kent TN2 3DR

Reprinted 1998

ISBN 0 85532 810 X

Printed in Spain by Elkar S. Coop. Bilbao 48012

Page 1
Natural basket
see also page 33

Page 3
Orange-net bowl
see also page 79

Opposite
Newspaper bread basket
*A step-by-step project shown on
pages 15–18*

Contents

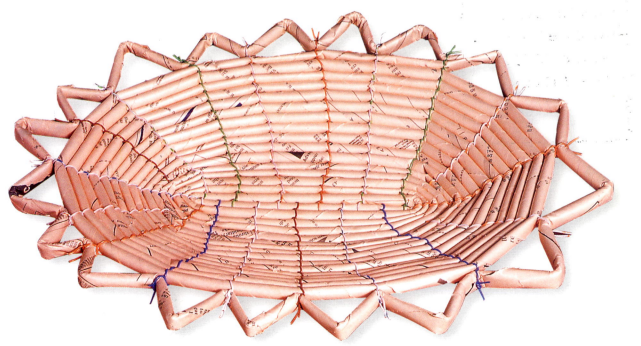

Introduction

There is nothing new about making baskets using materials that are to hand; it is what people have been doing all over the world for thousands of years, and it is one of the reasons why baskets are so diverse in shape and form. In northern Europe, we use the stems and branches of our indigenous shrubs and trees; in Scandinavia, birch forests provide bark and tree roots; in South East Asia, there is an abundance of bamboo and cane; and in the dry American Southwest and parts of Africa, grasses are utilised. Of course, these are generalisations, but the form of a basket tends to be determined by the materials being used and the basket's intended use.

If the material is long and tapered, as with willow, the woven method known as stake and strand predominates. This technique employs the varying thickness of natural materials to best advantage, utilising strong rods as stakes or uprights and the finer material as weavers, to infill between the stakes. The resulting baskets are generally strong and rugged in appearance.

Some materials, such as bamboo and cane, are long and regular in shape and can be split into even strands, so the plaiting technique is favoured. With this method there is no distinction between stakes and weavers and, as the materials are of the same thickness, the resulting baskets tend to be regular in shape and have a smooth surface texture, often with obvious corners and points.

Grasses tend to be short and fine, so they are usually bunched and bound tightly into coils. This coiling technique tends to produce rounded forms, and a decorative element is often found in the stitching.

Stake and strand, plaiting and coiling are the three main techniques that can be identified in baskets made all over the world. They are also the ones that I will be demonstrating in this book, because the materials that I am using lend themselves to one or other, or a combination of these techniques.

I live in a city where man-made materials are more readily available than natural ones. Most of them come into the house as food packaging. Man-made materials come in many forms and, consequently, they are suitable for coiling, plaiting and stake and strand. Recycled materials are often very colourful and, as with most natural materials, if you collect them yourself they are free. All that is required is a little effort to collect them, some simple rules for preparation . . . and you can begin.

Materials and tools

When working with recycled materials, quantity is all important – basically, the more the better. You need to have sufficient for the item you are going to make, together with some more that you can experiment with. I am a hoarder of potential materials; often, I gather them with no particular project in mind, but knowing that when the time comes I will have exactly what I need for my basket or bowl.

You probably already have most of the tools needed for making baskets from recycled materials. There are no complicated or expensive pieces of essential equipment necessary, but a power drill and a hot-glue gun could prove helpful for some of the projects.

An assortment of recycled materials
The possibilities are endless . . . paper, cardboard, plastic bottles and bags, corks, bottle tops and caps, strapping tape, wire, leaves and fabric.

Materials

Corrugated cardboard is strong and flexible. It can be cut into strips and used for plaiting, coiling and stake and strand. It also has a good surface to paint on.

Pressed card, as in cereal packets, often has colourful printing. Although not as strong as corrugated cardboard, it is useful for plaiting.

Juice and milk cartons are strong, colourful and flexible, with the added bonus of being waterproof. Cut on a spiral, to get long strips, they are ideal for plaiting and weaving.

Newspapers, magazines, old bank statements, love letters, old books, wallpaper, catalogues, and telephone directories can be rolled for coiling, or folded for plaiting.

Plastic and polythene bottles cut on a spiral into long strips can be woven or plaited. Cut downwards, into vertical strips, they can form the structure of a stake and strand basket.

Plastic strapping tapes are ideal for plaiting and weaving.

Plastic carrier bags can be cut into lengths for weaving or making ropes.

Metal drinks cans can be cut into strips and woven with other materials. You do need to be cautious when handling cut metal.

Metal bottle tops can be used as decoration.

Wire can be used for stitching, lacing and weaving. The plastic coating stripped off wire by scrap merchants, is useful for stitching and weaving.

Corks can be pierced and then threaded on to string or wire for coiling.

Natural materials such as iris and montbretia leaves, grape vine, pine needles, lavender or rosemary twigs, brambles and long grasses are all suitable for coiling.

Shells and driftwood make attractive edges and handles.

Fabrics, clothes, tights and roller blinds can all be cut into long strips for weaving and coiling.

Tools

There are only two essential tools for making all the items in this book – something to cut with and something to pierce with. However, there are a number of other tools which, although not essential, will make things quicker and easier for you.

1. **Power or hand drill** for drilling holes in corks and driftwood.
2. **Glue gun** for quick gluing of cardboard (pva glues will also work).
3. **Bodkin**, awl, skewer or steel knitting needle for piercing holes.
4. **Craft knife** for cutting card.
5. **Kitchen knife** (this is only required for cutting corks).
6. **Hole punch** for making holes in plastic and useful for when a neat hole is required.
7. **Stapler** for holding things together temporarily.
8. **Pliers** for bending or cutting wire.
9. **Side cutters** for cutting and trimming wire.
10. **Clothes pegs** for holding work in progress (I also use some small spring-loaded metal clamps).
11. **Clippers** or strong household scissors for general cutting of paper, card, plastic and fabric.
12. **Pencils** and pens.
13. **Compasses** (a large pair is most useful).
14. **Paint brushes** and sponges for decorating the materials.
15. **Steel ruler** used in conjunction with the craft knife for cutting straight strips.
16. **Tape measure**.

Preparing materials

Preparing the materials is not difficult and is based on the general principle of trying to make the longest strips possible. This task can often seem a chore, especially when you want to get on with making something. However, it pays to take your time and prepare thoroughly – your efforts will be rewarded.

When cutting strips, try to ensure that they are of equal width over their whole length. This is most evident in plaited work where straight, even-width strips will be rewarded with a regular-shaped basket.

Cardboard boxes can be opened out flat and painted before cutting into strips. Painting can be done using brushes, rollers or sponges – left-over household emulsion paint is ideal for use on card. If you are going to plait with your card strips, you can afford to be as adventurous as you like with your painting. When the painted card strips have been woven they will look quite different.

Plastic bags and bottles, juice cartons and tins can all be cut on a spiral to make strips of whatever width you like.

Natural materials, such as leaves and grasses, must be dried for storage and then dampened again when you want to use them.

A selection of prepared cardboard strips
Be adventurous with painted designs – use swirls, checks, dots, straight lines and solid colour – when assembled, the effect can be quite startling.

Coiling

Coiling is a method of making baskets that has been in existence since at least 2000BC. Remnants of coiled baskets often made with grasses, have been found in burial sites in desert areas of the world and some have been carbon-dated to prehistoric times.

The technique can produce forms such as a beehive, made from straw and bound with bramble, or an elegant platter, made with grasses and roots by native Americans and Africans.

Although you work in a spiral fashion, you can create square, oval, rectangular or triangular shapes, as well as round ones – in fact, by varying the base shape almost any form is possible.

Newspaper bread basket

This bread basket is made from rolled-up spills of newspaper, which are then coiled and connected with lengths of fine, plastic-coated telephone wire. The rolled spills are usually wider at one end than the other which enables them to be joined by simply pushing one into another. Decide on the size of the basket you want to make before you start cutting wires.

You will need

- *Several sheets of newspaper*
- *Telephone wire or strong string, cut in lengths that are one-and-a-half times longer than the intended width of the basket*
- *Glue gun or paper glue*
- *Scissors*
- *Ruler and pencil*

1. Tear broadsheet newspapers in half.

2. Start in a corner and roll up a sheet as tight as possible to form a spill.

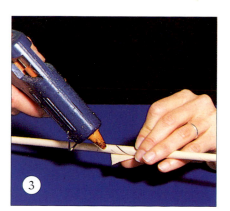

3. Use a glue gun or paper glue to secure the final flap to the spill.

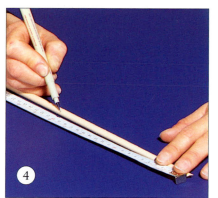

4. Make two pencil marks on the spill, 5cm (2in) and 20cm (8in) down from the narrow end.

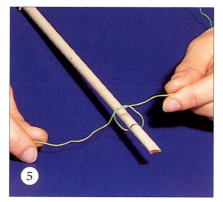

5. Tie lengths of wire round the spill, 1cm (½in) apart, making the first knot at the 5cm (2in) mark.

6. Turn alternate knots round so that six are on one side of the spill and six are on the other.

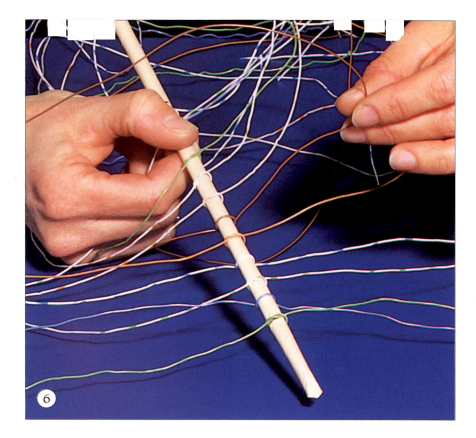

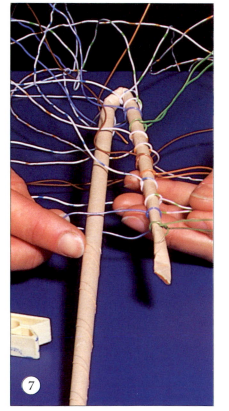

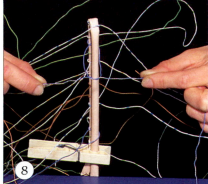

7. Fold the spill back on itself at the twelfth knot. Arrange the wires that are knotted on the inside of the first length of the spill, over and under the second length.

8. Clamp the folded spill with a peg and start knotting the wire round the second length.

9. Tuck in the 5cm (2in) raw end before tying the last knot.

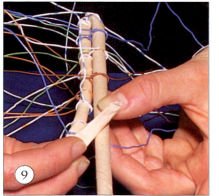

10. Fold the spill over the top of the first length and then knot down the third length using the other set of wires.

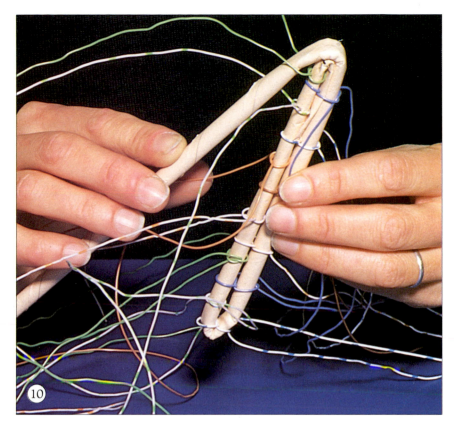

11. Add another spill by sliding its narrow end inside the hole in the first spill.

12. Add an extra length of wire at each end of the folded spill.

13. Start to shape the basket by offsetting the next and subsequent lengths of spill while you are knotting them. Add extra wires around the ends of the basket as necessary.

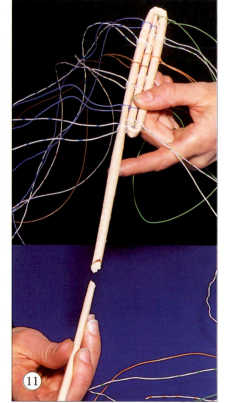

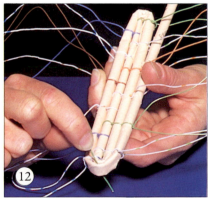

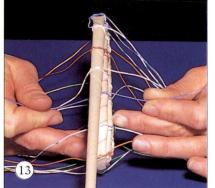

14. Continue joining lengths of spills and knotting them in place. When the bread basket is large enough, stop knotting at a point that is opposite the first knot.

15. Now work the border design. Fold the spill to form a triangular shape and knot its second fold with the next set of wires.

16. Continue round the edge of the basket to create the zig-zag border.

17. When the border is complete, cut off the excess spill. Finally, trim the ends of the knotted wires leaving a decorative twist of approximately 1cm (½in) on each.

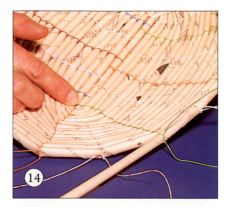

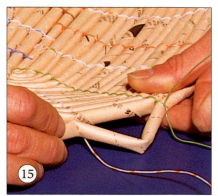

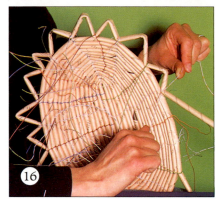

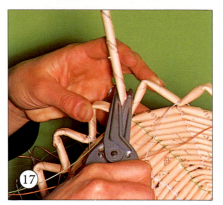

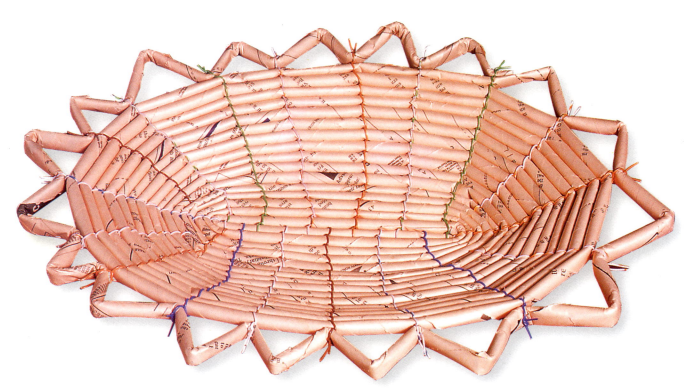

The finished bread basket
To preserve the colour and appearance of this basket, and to make it easy to keep clean, apply an acrylic lacquer.

Cork bowl

This bowl is made with just a metal jar lid, some corks, small bits of driftwood and bottle tops. It could be used on the table for bread or fruit, or in the bathroom.

I used some small pieces of driftwood and metal bottle tops for the final edging of this bowl. However, you could change the appearance of the edging by using other materials.

You will need
- *Metal jar lid*
- *Approximately thirty corks*
- *Small pieces of driftwood*
- *Metal bottle tops*
- *Fine wire or strong fishing line*
- *Bodkin or awl*
- *Large-bladed kitchen knife*
- *Drill*
- *Pliers*

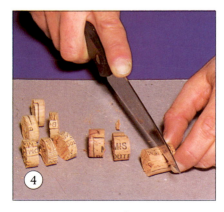

1. Use a bodkin to pierce sixteen equidistant holes in the lid, approximately 5mm (¼in) in from the outer edge.

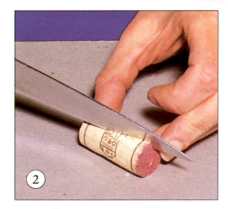

2. Use a large-bladed knife to cut one cork in half at an angle.

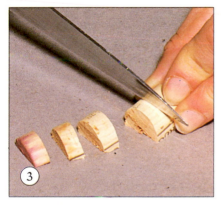

3. Cut one of the tapered pieces into six slices.

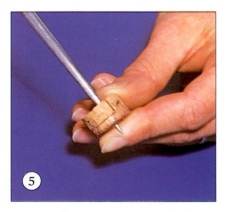

4. Cut two more corks into six round slices and the rest of the corks into four round slices.

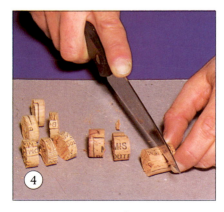

5. Use a bodkin to pierce a hole through the middle of all the cork slices.

6. Thread fine wire through the hole in the shaped slices of cork, starting with the smallest piece. Next, thread on the corks cut into sixths and, finally, all the quartered corks, to form a long string.

7. Knot another length of wire (for binding) and thread it through one hole in the lid so that the knot is on the underside. Now take the wire between the first two slices of cork, over the core wire, and back through the next hole in the lid.

8. Continue passing the binding wire between the slices of tapered cork and through consecutive holes in the lid.

9. When you have secured one round of cork to the lid, link the second round to the first by threading the binding wire over the core wire between adjacent corks.

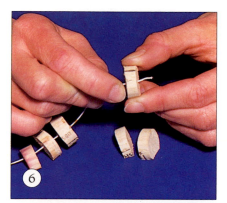

10. Tie on more binding wire as it runs out with a neat reef knot. Trim off the ends so that the knot will be hidden between the slices of cork.

11. Continue building up the spiral of corks until the bowl is large enough. Finish the basket by binding on more tapered corks to match the taper at the start; this will ensure that the outer rim is level and circular in shape.

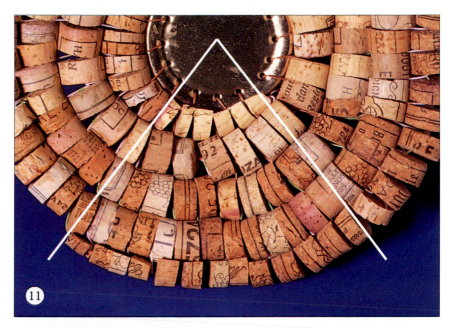

12. Drill a small hole in each end of the pieces of driftwood for the inner ring of border decoration.

13. Loop a short length of wire between two cork slices and pass both ends through one of the holes in the driftwood. Use another short length of wire to secure the other end. Repeat for the other pieces of the inner ring.

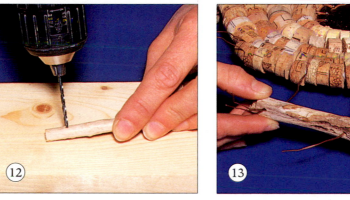

14. Arrange the outer bridging ring of driftwood around the bowl. Mark the drilling positions on each piece to align with the holes in the inner ring. Pass the wires through the holes and secure in place with a small knot. Trim the wire approximately 100mm (4in) from the knot.

15. Partially squeeze the sides of the bottle tops as shown – you could use a screwdriver instead of your thumb.

16. Scrunch up the wires protruding from the driftwood, place them in a bottle top and then squeeze the bottle top tightly with a pair of pliers to trap the wires.

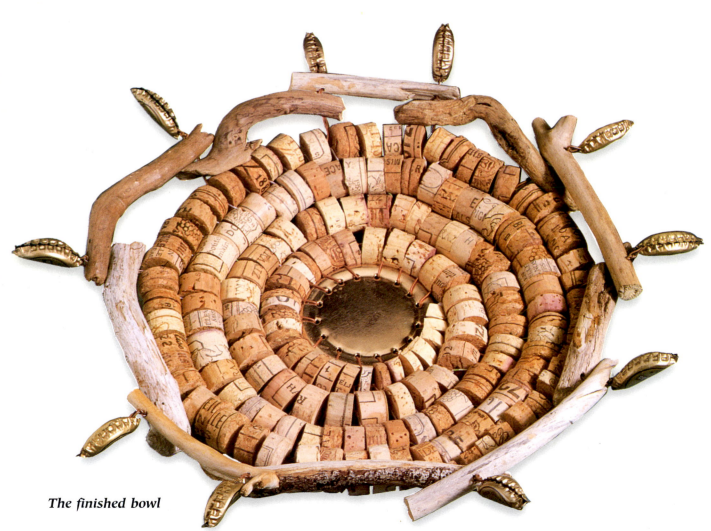

The finished bowl

22

Card fruit basket

This basket is made round a square-shaped base. However, you can alter the shape of the basket simply by changing the shape of the base – everything else remains the same.

You will need

- *Painted corrugated cardboard cut from two or more boxes*
- *Assortment of plastic bags*
- *Sharp dressmaking scissors*
- *Glue gun or fast acting adhesive*
- *Bodkin or awl*
- *Craft knife*
- *Steel ruler*
- *Darning needle*
- *Pencil*
- *Small circular lid or container*

1. Cut the plastic bags into strips with dressmaking scissors. Trim off the bottom of the bag and then start to cut a long taper from one edge, to get the spiral going.

2. When the taper is 4cm (1½in) wide, continue to cut round the bag to produce a long strip of equal width.

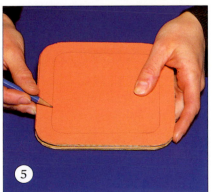

3. Draw two 15cm (6in) squares on pieces of painted cardboard. Use a small circular lid or container as a guide to round off the corners of the square.

4. Cut out the shapes with a craft knife and glue the two pieces together. The base will be more rigid if you place the corrugations in the pieces at right angles to each other.

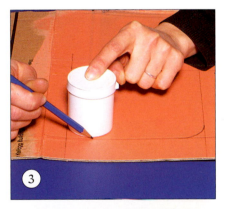

5. Draw a pencil line all round the base, 2cm (¾in) in from the edge.

6. Use a bodkin to pierce approximately twenty-four equidistant holes round the pencil line.

23

7. Use a steel ruler and a craft knife to cut a large sheet of painted cardboard into 5cm (2in) wide strips. The corrugations should lie across the width of each strip.

8. Use the blunt ends of a pair of clippers or scissors to score a line down the centre of the unpainted side of each strip.

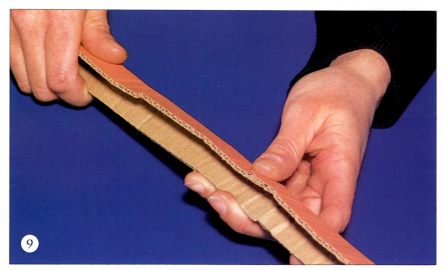

10. Soften the strips by squeezing and bending them between your fingers and thumbs.

9. Fold each strip along the scored line, so that the painted surface is on the outside.

11. Cut a taper, equal to the length of one side of the square base, in the end of one of the folded strips.

12. Tie a knot in the end of a plastic-bag strip and thread the other end on to a large-eyed darning needle. Sandwich the base inside the tapered strip. Use a simple overstitch to bind the tapered edge of the strip to the base.

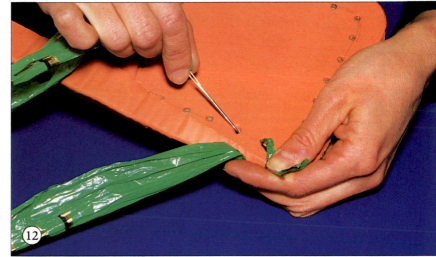

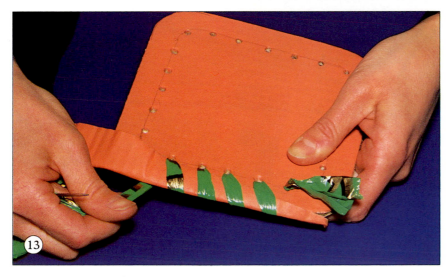

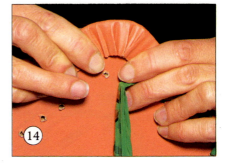

14. Squeeze the cardboard strip round the corner of the base by pushing rather than stretching it.

13. Work along the first side keeping the stitches as neat as possible.

15. Work round the four sides of the base. When you get back to the first corner, use the bodkin to make more holes. Place the holes slightly to one side of the plastic thread, approximately 1cm (½in) from the inner edge of the sewn strip.

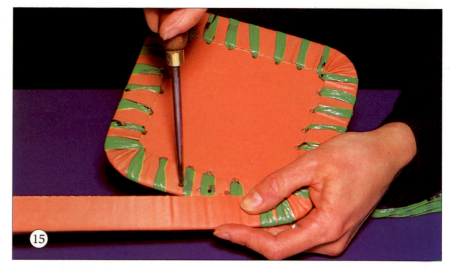

16. When the thread runs out, tie on a new length with a small knot. Position the knot over the folded edge of the card strip so that it will be hidden by subsequent layers.

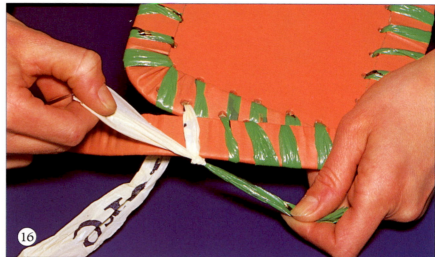

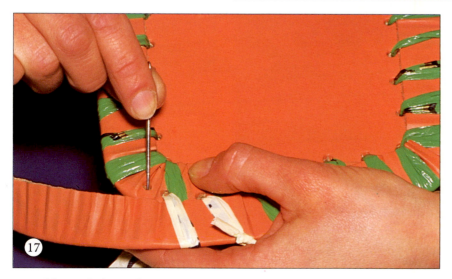

17. Add extra holes at the corners to maintain an even spacing of the stitches.

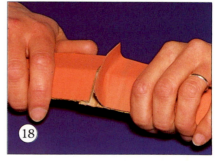

18. When you need to join cardboard strips, separate the layers of one length, apply glue to both inside surfaces, tuck in a new length and then fold back the glued flaps to secure.

19. Continue sewing round the bowl, angling the layers to create shape. Finish the bowl on the same side as the start point. Taper the end of the last strip to make a flat-topped bowl.

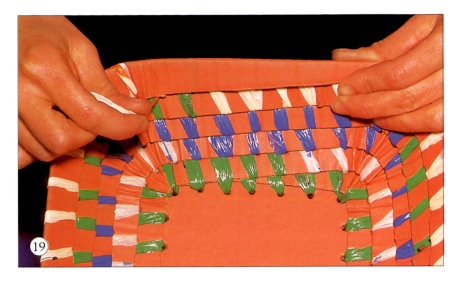

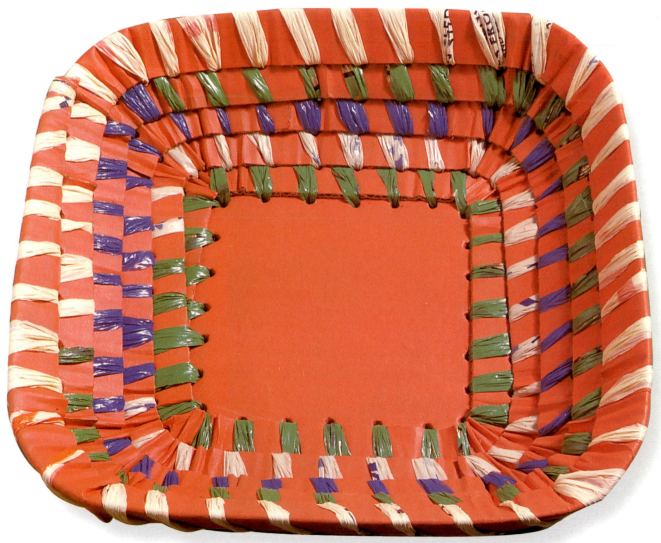

The finished basket

Card laundry basket

This basket uses the same technique as the fruit basket on pages 23–7, but on a larger scale – for this basket I used five large cardboard boxes.

You can use almost any type of fabric as long as it is not too heavy. If you are using an item of clothing, cut the fabric into strips in the same way as the plastic bag on page 23; if you are using a flat piece of fabric, cut it as shown in this project.

You will need
- *Painted cardboard cut into 12cm (4¾in) wide strips*
- *Assortment of fabric*
- *Plastic bottle cap*
- *Glue gun or fast-acting glue*
- *Dressmaker's scissors*
- *All-purpose scissors*
- *Bodkin or bradawl*
- *Darning needle*
- *Craft knife and steel rule*
- *Tape measure*
- *Compass and pencil*

1. Use a sharp pair of dressmaker's scissors to cut the corners of the pieces of fabric into smooth curves.

2. Work from an outer edge and cut the fabric in a spiral, to make a continuous strip of equal width.

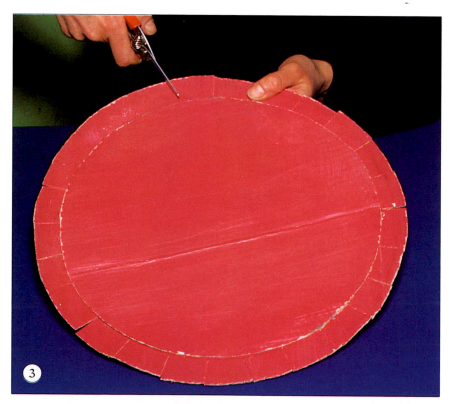

3. Cut a 40cm (16in) diameter circle from a piece of painted cardboard. Draw another circle 4cm (1½in) in from the edge and then make a series of cuts, about 5cm (2in) apart, in to the inner circle.

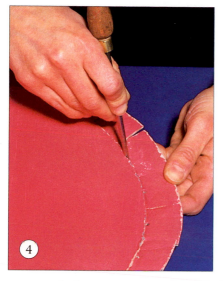

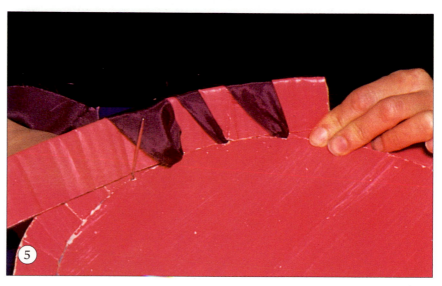

4. Pierce holes round the drawn circle, in the centre of each segment.

5. Prepare the 12cm (4¾in) wide strips of cardboard as shown on page 24. Knot one end of the fabric strip, thread the other end on to a darning needle and start to sew the cardboard strip to the base.

6. Sew the board strips round and round, in a similar manner to that shown on page 25, making the side of the basket taper outwards slightly. Join fabric and cardboard strips as they run out (see page 26).

7. When you want to start reducing the diameter of the basket, squeeze the cardboard strip as shown and angle it inward as you sew it into position.

8. Continue reducing the diameter. As the angle of the strips becomes more acute, you will have to hold them firmly in place as you sew.

9. Cut a long taper in the end of the last strip and sew it down to form a flat top. Finish with a neat knot on the inside.

10. Next, make a lid for the basket. Measure the diameter of the opening at the top of the basket. Cut two circles of painted cardboard, approximately 5cm (2in) larger than the opening, and glue them back to back (see page23). Cut a folded strip of cardboard long enough to go round the circumference with a 5cm (2in) overlap. Sew the edge strip round the circle of cardboard, using the technique on pages 25.

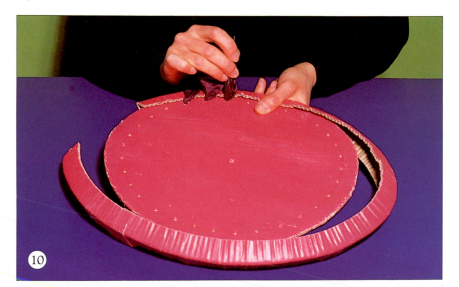

11. Peel back the top layer from one end of the edging strip and cut away the bottom layers.

12. Apply glue to the end of the edging strip and make an overlapping join. Continue stitching over the top to complete the rim.

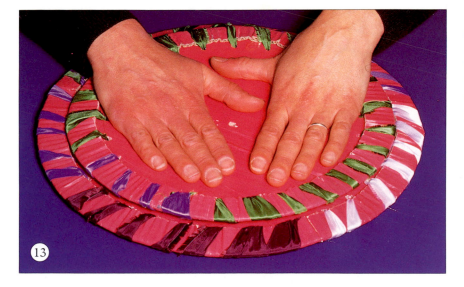

13. Repeat stages 10–12 to make another cardboard circle. Make it slightly smaller than the diameter of the opening in the top of the basket. Glue the small circle in the middle of the large one and apply pressure until the glue has set.

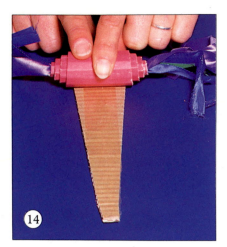

14. Now make a handle. Cut a 50cm (20in) length of cardboard, 10cm (4in) wide, and taper it to a blunt point. Glue a few strips of ribbon or fabric to the wide end. Roll the strip into a sausage shape and glue the end to secure.

15. Use a darning needle to pass the ribbons on one side of the handle through the centre of the lid.

16. Pierce two holes in a plastic bottle cap, pass a ribbon through each hole and tie a knot to secure the handle.

The finished laundry basket

Round basket

Painted cardboard and plastic bags are used on a round base to make this variation of the fruit basket (see page 27).

Natural basket

Coiled montbretia leaves, bound together with string, are used for this basket. It is finished with a rim of cork segments.

Overleaf
Driftwood basket

Coiled offcuts of cane are used to make a basket with a driftwood edge.

Shell basket

Corks are coiled round a cheese box and the basket is given an oyster and scallop shell edge.

33

Plaiting

Plaiting is a term commonly applied to weaving with materials of a similar thickness and size, where there is no distinction made between the warp and the weft.

Plaiting is used a lot in baskets that originate in the far east where they are often made of rattan or bamboo which splits readily into even strips. Elements can be woven in different patterns; over one and under one, or over and under two or more strips at a time.

One of the characteristics of a plaited basket is that, although the base may be square or rectangular, the top will automatically form into a round or oval shape unless it has been deliberately creased to create angles.

Card waste paper basket

This is a very useful and strong basket. It is made from plaited, painted cardboard and decorated with painted strips that are cut from a plastic bottle.

You will need

- *Thirteen strips of corrugated cardboard 4cm (1½in) wide and 120 cm (47 in) long*
- *Six plastic bottles*
- *Paint*
- *Acrylic lacquer*
- *Scissors*
- *Stapler*
- *Paint brushes*
- *Sponge*
- *Bodkin or awl*
- *Ruler*
- *Clothes pegs*

1. Mark the centre point on two strips and then position the cardboard strips at right angles with the marks adjacent to each other. Use a clothes peg to hold the strips together.

2. Add more strips, weaving them over and under each other to form a square, six strips by six strips.

3. When all twelve strips are in place, staple the four corners of the square.

4. Turn the 'fabric' of woven strips over and use the blunt end of a pair of scissors to score diagonal lines between the midpoint of each side of the square.

5. Bend up the triangle of weave along the scored lines to form the start of the sides of the basket.

6. New corners are formed at the points where the scored lines meet. Lift up the weavers at either side and cross them at right angles, so that the woven sequence of overs and unders is maintained. Peg them in position.

7. Bring up more strips from the folded-up sides and weave them together. Take your time while weaving these strips, and keep using pegs to hold the fabric together. Go back over areas of weave to tighten it and maintain a neat squared pattern.

8. Carry on weaving with all the strips, working round the basket. Notice that the shape changes to a cylindrical form.

9. When the basket is tall enough, recheck the tightness of the weave and peg all crossovers. Now draw a line across the diagonals of the woven strips; if the weave is tight, the line will be horizontal.

10. Cut round the drawn line, one section at a time, and staple just below the line as you go.

11. Decorate the basket by sponging on a coat of acrylic paint. When the paint is dry, apply one or two coats of varnish to strengthen the basket.

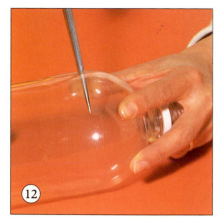

12. Pierce a hole just below the round neck of a plastic bottle and cut off the top.

13. Start with a taper and cut round the straight body of the bottle in a spiral to obtain a long strip 2cm (¾in) wide.

14. Tape down the plastic strip temporarily and decorate one side with acrylic paints.

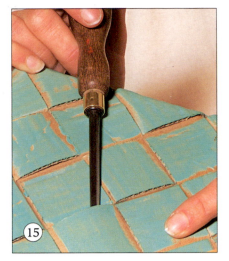

15. Use a bradawl to open up any parts of the fabric that have become stuck together with paint or varnish.

16. Weave the decorated plastic strip through the woven fabric of the basket.

17. Cut another strip of plastic, 6mm (¼in) wide. Paint it and then use this to sew on a card rim round the top of the basket, using a similar method to that shown on page 31. Finally, cut a wider strip of plastic and thread it round the rim, under the stitching.

The finished basket

Card letter tray

Many cardboard boxes have colourful printing. When you cut strips from printed boxes and then plait with them, some very decorative effects can be achieved. This letter tray is made from a couple of boxes printed with the same bold design.

You will need

- *Strips of card, 4cm (1½in) wide:*
  Ten strips 50cm (20in) long
  Eight strips 43cm (17in) long
  One strip 140cm (55in) long
- *Packing tape, approximately 5.5m (17ft) long*
- *Scissors*
- *Stapler*
- *Bodkin or awl*
- *Clothes pegs*

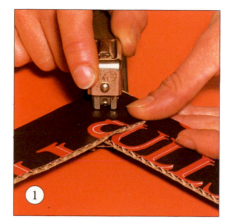

1. Staple the corners of one 50cm (20in) strip and one 43cm (17in) strip together at right angles.

2. Weave in two more of the same strips and staple their ends to the first two strips.

3. Continue weaving the remaining strips to make a rectangle, ten strips by eight, stapling their overlapping ends to the first two strips. Tighten the weave before stapling the overlapping ends of the last two strips. Trim off any card sticking out beyond the weaving.

4. Cut diagonally through the two layers of card at each corner of the rectangle and discard the small triangular shapes.

5. Overlap the triangular ends of the strips to make the corners.

6. Staple the corner pieces together. Repeat stages 4–6 at the other three corners. Trim off the little points.

7. Make two holes in each segment round the top edge and sew on a rim in a similar way to that shown on page 31. Split the packing tape to a width of approximately 6mm (¼in) and use this as the binding.

Letter trays
You can vary the colour scheme to produce a different effect.

Juice-carton glasses case

This project uses an effective combination of material and technique to produce a strong, flexible and water-proof glasses case. The bright summer colours are ideal for sunglasses.

You will need

- *Eight strips of juice carton 1.5cm (½in) wide and 80cm (31½in) long (cut the carton in a spiral as shown for the plastic bottles on page 40)*
- *Scissors*
- *Masking tape*
- *Ruler*
- *Clothes pegs*

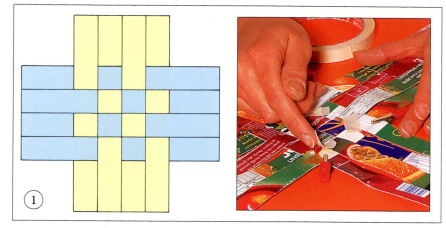

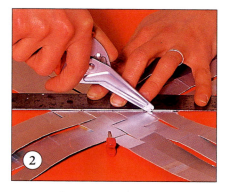

1. Follow the diagram and weave eight carton strips to form a four-by-four square. Attach small pieces of masking tape to hold the strips together.

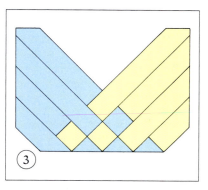

2. Turn the strips over (silver side uppermost) and use blunt-ended scissors to score diagonally across the square.

3. Fold along the scored line (silver side on the inside); the bottom left-hand strip should be on top of the weave as shown.

4. Fold the lowest right-hand strip on the front, back on itself.

Note

When weaving the initial four-by-four-strip square it is possible to make two different arrangements. One of these is shown in the diagram at stage 1 which, when folded in stage 3, will have the bottom left-hand strip on top. If your folded woven square has the bottom right-hand strip on top, you must adapt the instructions so that the words 'right' and 'right hand' read 'left' and 'left hand' respectively, and vice versa.

5. Crease the exposed lower strip at 45° and lay it parallel to the strips pointing to the left.

6. Weave the strip over, under and over the upper three strips that point to the right, and then lay the first right-hand strip back in its original position.

7. Turn the piece over and repeat stages 4–6. Do not weave through the lower sets of strips.

8. Move to the left-hand side, crease the single bottom strip at 45° and then weave it through the strips pointing to the left. Turn the piece over and repeat this stage with the remaining single strip. Use pegs to hold the work as necessary. Repeat stages 4–8 until the case is long enough.

9. Draw a line across the diagonals of the weave where you want the top to be. Release the weaving at the points, down to the line, so that there are five strips on top pointing to the right, and three underneath pointing to the left. It may be necessary to adjust the line, one row up or one row down, to get the configuration of strips shown here.

10. Start one strip in from the right and crease a pair of strips at 45° to form a horizontal edge.

11. Move to the left and fold down the next pair in a similar way.

12. Cut a taper on the end of the lower right-hand strip and tuck it into the weave of the case.

13. Work round the top of the case, folding down pairs of strips and tucking in the right-hand ones until all strips have been woven into the case. At the corners, open up shape to make the folding and tucking easier.

14. Trim off the remaining lengths of strips to complete the case.

The finished glasses case

Newspaper wall basket

This simple basket, made from folded sheets of newspaper, could be hung in the kitchen and used for storing wooden spoons, clothes pegs or plastic bags, or it could be used in the bathroom as a waste bin. It could also work as a wall hanger for a pot plant.

You will need

- *Seven broadsheets of newspaper*
- *Wire coat hanger*
- *Scissors*
- *Clothes pegs*
- *Round-nosed pliers*
- *Wire cutters or ordinary pliers*

1. Fold the long edge of a sheet of newspaper into the middle and then fold the opposite edge into the middle.

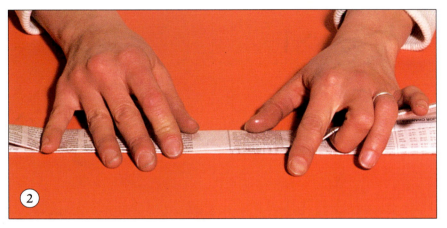

2. Continue folding the sheet until it is 8cm (3in) wide, and then fold it in half. Hold the strip with a clothes peg. Make seven of these strips.

3. Twist one strip to form a tight cone and clip the two loose ends together with a peg.

4. Add six strips as weavers, alternating them over/under and under/over the two vertical ends of the first strip.

5. Lift the first pair of weavers and cross them as shown.

6. Hold the strips in place with your thumb and continue to lift pairs of strips and weave them into shape.

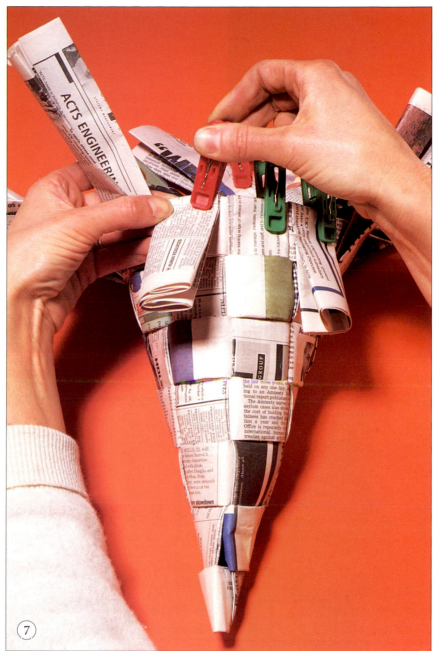

7. When all strips have been woven in, turn the piece so that the horizontal weave is facing you and tighten the weave. Turn the flaps over the top edge and secure each flap with a peg.

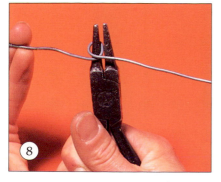

8. Cut a coat hanger to get a long length of wire. Use a pair of round-nosed pliers to make a small loop in the middle of the length of wire.

9. Use the woven basket as a guide and bend the wire to fit round the folded edge, allowing an overlap of about a strip's width.

10. Work from the wire loop and unclip the flaps folded into the middle. Pull them over the wire and tuck the ends through the outside weave to secure. You may find it easier to fold the end of each flap into a point.

11. Now go back round the rim, folding the other flaps over the wire and tucking them into the inside weave. Trim off the excess paper.

The finished wall basket

Overleaf
Wall-hung laundry basket
This unusually-shaped basket is made from painted corrugated cardboard and strapping tape. Each strip is cut to shape to make the arc form.

Selection of plaited cardboard baskets
The dish shapes are created by pre-cutting the card strips so that they are narrower at each end. All the other shapes are made with parallel strips of card.

Stake and strand

The basketry that comes from this method of weaving is distinguishable by the fact that there is a distinct warp and weft – the warp being the stakes which provide the skeleton, and the weft being the strands which provide the flesh. The stakes are usually stronger and spaced further apart than the thinner, more pliable strands. This technique is most commonly used in Britain and much of northern Europe, where willow is the main material. There is no limit to the variety of shapes that can be created with stake and strand weaving and in this respect it is probably the most versatile of the techniques that I outline.

Plastic-bottle pencil holder

This is a good project for learning basic pairing weave and colour patterns. The techniques described here can be used in lots of other ways. For example, you can use the plastic-bottle stakes as the basic structure for other shapes of containers; you can change the pattern of the weave by using an even number of stakes; and you can use the weaving techniques with stakes made from other materials.

You will need

- *Two identical plastic bottles*
- *Two plastic bags of different colours. Cut them into strips as shown on page 23.*
- *Scissors*
- *Bodkin or awl*

1. Cut the top off two plastic bottles (see page 40), and then cut one of them into fifteen roughly equal strips (stakes). Insert the uncut bottle inside the cut one to act as a former.

2. Lay a red plastic strand in behind one stake and out through the next gap. Lay a black plastic strand behind the stake to the left and out over the red strand.

3. Work to the right and weave the black strand over one stake and behind the next.

4. Now weave the red strand over the black, in front of one stake and behind the next.

5. Continue weaving the red and black strands round the bottle. When you start the second row, you will see how the pattern starts to develop.

6. When one of the strands starts to run out, lay in a new length of the same colour behind a stake and continue weaving with the new length. The short lengths can be trimmed off later.

7. When the pattern is as high as you want it to be, replace the red strand with a second black strand and work a border with a couple of rows of solid black.

8. Cut the ends of the stakes into points.

9. Insert a bodkin through a few layers of weaving and bring the point out just below the top row. Fold a pointed stake over and push it through the weave behind the bodkin.

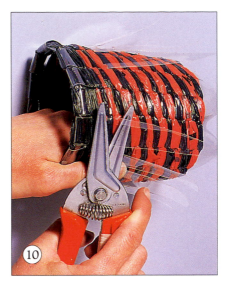

10. When all the stakes have been inserted into the weave, trim off the pointed ends.

11. Remove the inner bottle former and cut it to the same height as the woven one. Place a square of black plastic over the rounded end of the bottle and insert the bottle back into the woven bowl.

Plastic-bottle pencil holders
The finished project (above) and a variation (left) which is made with the same pairing weave, but over an even number of stakes.

Card and plastic shoulder bag

This bag is made using a combination of techniques. The base is plaited with strips cut from cardboard boxes. When the strips are folded up round a former they become the stakes for the stake and strand technique. The stakes are then woven with packing tape to form the sides. There are many other materials you could use instead of tape – strips of fabric, plastic bags, juice cartons to name a few.

You will need

- *Nine strips of painted and varnished card, 80cm (31½in) long and 4cm (1½in) wide*
- *Cardboard box*
- *Approximately seventeen lengths of packing tape, at least 80cm (31½in) long*
- *Selection of plastic carrier bags*
- *String*
- *Scissors*
- *Stapler*
- *Bodkin or awl*
- *Darning needle*
- *Tape measure*
- *Large elastic band (I make my own with strips cut from an old pair of tights)*

1. Plait nine strips of card to make a base six strips by three strips. Staple them together at the four corners.

2. Cut down a cardboard box to the same size as the base and, using this as a former, fold up the side stakes.

3. Hold the stakes round the former with a large elastic band or a strip cut from a pair of old tights. Then, starting at one corner, weave yellow packing tape through the stakes with a simple under-and-over sequence.

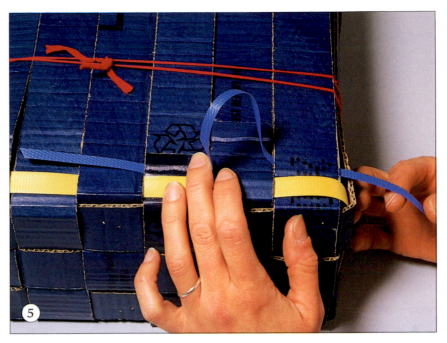

4. Overlap the tucked-in end of the tape, weave it through a few more stakes, and trim off the excess.

5. Start from a different point and weave a second row with narrow blue. Continue working up the basket using different colours and widths of tape. Stagger the start points of each row.

6. When the basket is deep enough, trim off the tops of the stakes approximately 2cm (¾in) above the last row of tape.

7. Use a bodkin to pierce two holes in each stake just above the last row of weaving.

8. Sew on an edging round the top of the basket (see page 25).

9. Split some tape down the middle to make very thin strips and use this to add a decorative weave through the middle of each stake. Work down one side, across the base and then up the other side. Tuck the loose ends under the border rim.

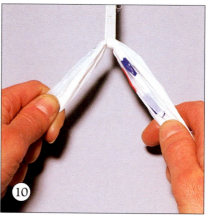

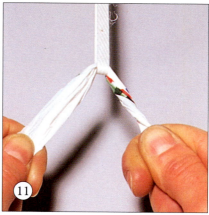

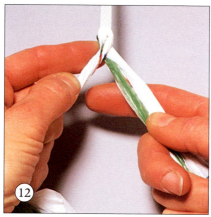

10. Now make the rope handles. Secure a loop of string to the leg of a chair and thread three plastic-bag strips through the loop.

11. Make a few clockwise twists in the right-hand length of plastic.

12. Hold both sides taut and change hands, crossing the twisted length over the untwisted length.

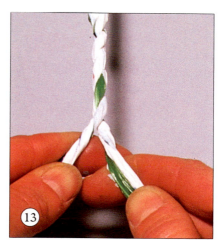

13. Now make a few clockwise twists in the new right-hand length and change hands again, crossing the right-hand twist over the left-hand one. Continue twisting and crossing, and lay in other strips as you run out. When the rope is long enough, knot the ends and remove from the string support. Make a second rope in the same way.

14. Thread a double length of plastic-bag strip through one of the stakes, just under the rim. Take it over the knotted end of one of the ropes and back through the stake to the inside. Tie a knot, trim off the excess and tuck the short ends up under the inside of the rim. Attach the other end of the rope in a similar way. Fix the second rope to the other side of the basket to complete the project.

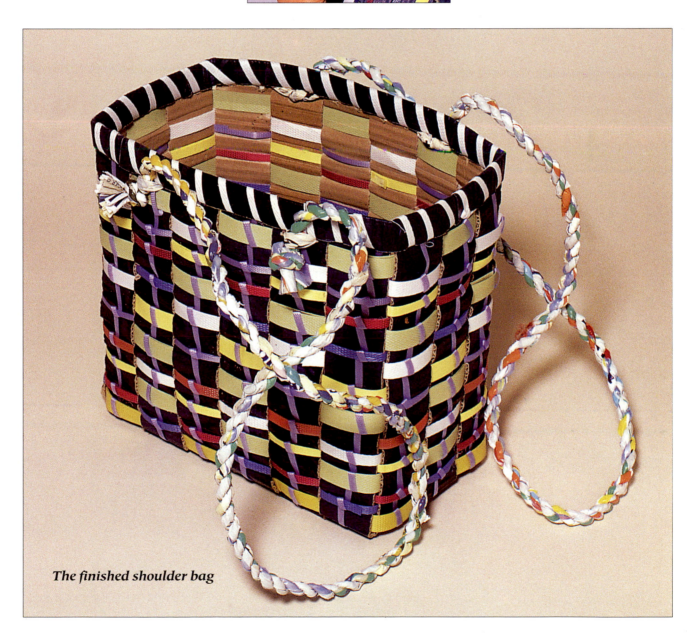

The finished shoulder bag

Iris leaf and card bowl

Instead of recycling dead plant leaves in the compost bin, you can use them to make this little basket for the table.

You will need
- *Approximately sixty iris leaves*
- *30cm (12in) square of cardboard*
- *Strong twine or cord*
- *Compass and pencil*
- *Tape measure*
- *Craft knife*
- *Steel ruler*
- *Towel*
- *Bodkin or awl*

1. Dry the iris leaves. Tie them in bundles and hang them in a dry, dark place for a couple of months.

2. The night before you wish to make the basket, wrap the bundle of leaves in a wet towel and leave them overnight to soften.

3. Draw two concentric circles on a piece of card, the outer one 270mm (10½in) diameter and the inner one 65mm (2½in) diameter. Divide the circle into fifteen equal segments, 24° apart, and draw lines as shown.

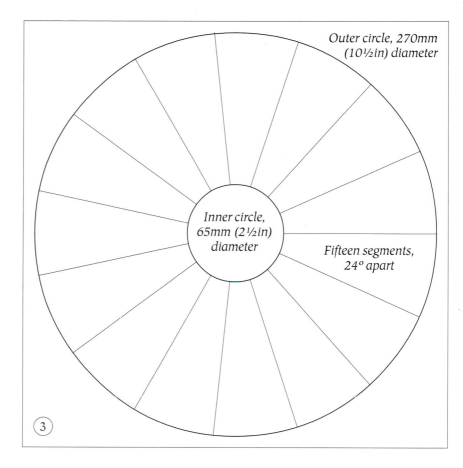

Outer circle, 270mm (10½in) diameter

Inner circle, 65mm (2½in) diameter

Fifteen segments, 24° apart

③

④

⑤

4. Make small pencil marks 20mm (¾in) to the left of each line and cut out triangular segments up to the inner circle.

5. Carefully soften and shape the stakes with your fingers and thumbs.

6. Turn the basket over so that you are working on the back. Start the weavers by laying the tips of two leaves round two adjacent stakes.

7. Use the pairing weave shown on page 55 to work the first row of leaves. Tuck the tip ends in as you work round to them.

8. Continue weaving, laying in new leaves tail-to-tail and tip-to-tip as necessary. Maintain tension and gently curve the stakes away from you as you work up the basket, so that the gap between the stakes closes.

9. When you reach the top of the stakes, prepare a cardboard rim (see page 25). Make two holes in each stake, thread a length of black cord and, using an overhand stitch, work round the rim in one direction. Tie a neat knot on the outside and trim off the excess cord. Thread another length of cord and finish the border by working round the rim in the opposite direction.

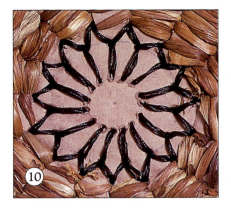

10. Finally, use the same cord to sew a decorative pattern on the cardboard base.

The finished iris leaf bowl

Left
Drinks-can basket
Several similar drinks cans are used for this basket. The sides are cut vertically to form stakes and are then woven with fine wire. Ring pulls are used to form the border.

Right
Laundry basket
This large piece is worked to a plan. All the plywood stakes are cut to shape first and then woven with a combination of willow and plastic-bag strips.

Shoulder-hung purse
This purse, which is large enough to take a cheque book, is made from plastic water bottles woven with plastic-bag strips (see page 57).

Plastic-bottle bowl
This black and white bowl is made from several plastic water bottles cut vertically to form stakes which arre then woven with plastic-bag strips.

Drinks-can-box basket
Made from drinks-can boxes and packing tape, this basket includes a combination of techniques – coiling for the shaped bowl, and stake and strand for the flat, top edge.

Drinks-can basket
You can create kinetic patterns by using several cans of the same pattern and aligning them carefully.

Assembly

This is not a recognised basketry technique although, confusingly, it is one that is used to make baskets. The Sussex trug is generally regarded as a basket and yet it employs no coiling or weaving – instead, the components are simply riveted and nailed together. Similar baskets can be found in Scandinavia. I use lacing, stitching and riveting to assemble baskets, some of which may also employ a recognised technique around the edges, such as coiling. Assembly is particularly appropriate for materials such as bottle tops which obviously cannot be cut into strips and woven.

Juice-carton bowl

This bowl is very quick to make and, by using cartons of the same design, a decorative pattern forms quite naturally. To make the bowl stand evenly, you must be precise when making the holes used to lace the cartons together.

You will need
- *Nine identical juice cartons*
- *Strong thread or cord*
- *Scissors*
- *Darning needle*
- *Hole punch, bodkin or awl*

1. Carefully pull apart the glued-down points of the juice cartons and then flatten the cartons.

2. Use a hole punch or a bodkin to make two holes in the same corner of each carton. It is important to make the holes at identical positions on each carton.

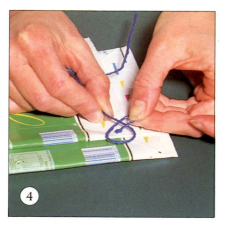

3. Overlap two cartons as shown, aligning the outer hole in the top carton with the inner hole in the bottom carton. Make a double knot in the end of a length of cord and thread it through the two holes.

4. Make a knot on top, pull the cord tight and make another knot under the first. Cut off excess cord.

5. Lay another carton underneath, align the holes and knot through them. Continue adding more cartons, and knot them together until all nine are linked in a row.

6. Arrange the cartons into a circular shape, and knot the first to the last with another length of cord.

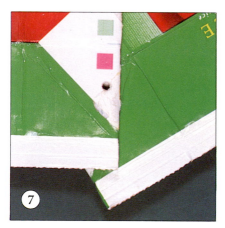

7. Overlap the corners of two adjacent cartons and pierce a hole through both cartons. Again, it is important that the holes are in the same place on each pair of cartons.

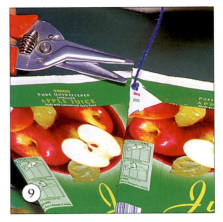

9. Finally, snip off the ends of the cord to leave neat knots.

8. Use the same knotting technique as in steps 3 and 4 to link all the outer edges together.

The finished juice-carton bowl

Bottle-cap bowl

This very practical bowl is fun to make because the dished shape is so easy to create. The bottle caps have a slight taper and, as you connect them together, the dished shape appears automatically.

You can make different shapes – a triangle, a hexagon or, as I have done for this project, a diamond shape.

You will need

- *Plastic bottle caps: forty-nine for the diamond thirty-six for the triangle thirty-seven for the hexagon*
- *Fine wire, strong cord or fishing line.*
- *Approximately 9m (30ft) of heavy-duty wire for the edging*
- *Bodkin*
- *Heavy-duty scissors or pliers*

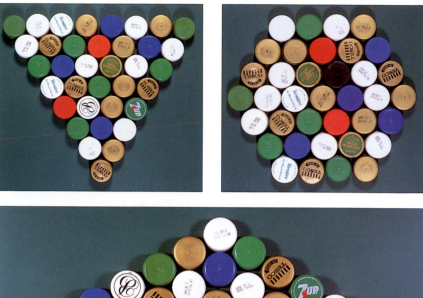

1. Arrange the caps in the shape you wish to make. Place the caps randomly, as I have done here, or in a definite pattern.

2. Use a bodkin to pierce six equi-distant holes in the top of each cap.

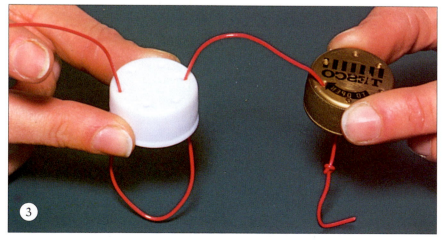

3. Knot a length of wire, take the other end up through a hole in cap 1 (see diagram), down through a hole in cap 2 and up through the opposite hole. Thread caps 3–7 in the same way.

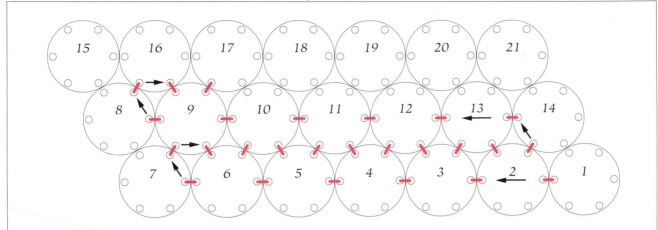

Connection diagram

Start at cap 1 and pass a wire through opposite holes down the first row to cap 7 (see stage 3).

Leave out cap 8 and work back up the row, linking caps 9–14 to caps 7–2 (see stage 4).

Thread the wire back down the second row, adding cap 8 on the end (see stage 5), and then link the caps in second and third rows as stage 4.

Repeat the procedure to link the other rows together, then, thread wire through the caps at the end of each row (see stage 6).

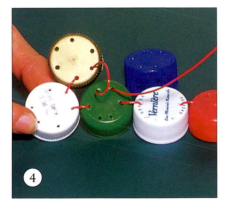

4. At cap 7, bring the wire up through an adjacent hole (not the opposite one) and take it down through a hole in cap 9 (cap 8 will be wired later). Continue linking the caps in the second row to those in the first row.

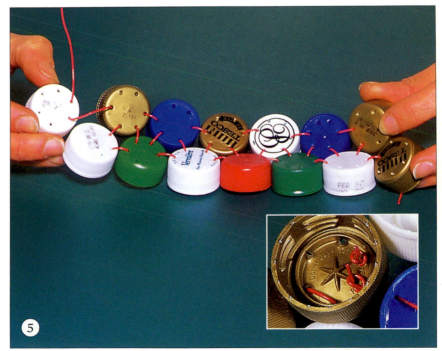

5. At the end of the second row, work back down the row taking the wire up and down through opposite holes. Add cap 8 to the end of the second row, bringing the wire up through an adjacent hole. When a length of wire runs out, tie it off with a neat knot, knot another length and then continue threading it through the caps.

6. When all the rows have been wired together, link the caps at the end of each row in a similar way.

7. Shape the heavy-duty wire round one of the acute corners of the diamond shape. Use a contrasting fine wire to bind an edging, taking the wire through the remaining holes in the caps.

On the second and subsequent rows, bind the fine wire round two rows of the heavy-duty wire. Finish at the point where you started with a neat knot.

The finished bottle-cap bowl

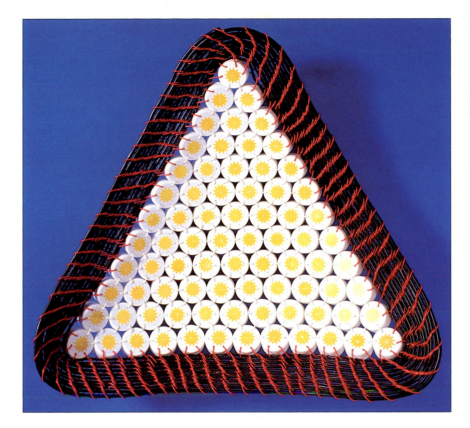

Triangular bottle-cap bowl
The brand of water bottle used for this piece has a sun printed on the top of the cap, and I decided to use it as part of the decoration. Having thought out the design, a considerable period of time elapsed before I could start to make the bowl – I had to drink sixty-six bottles of water!

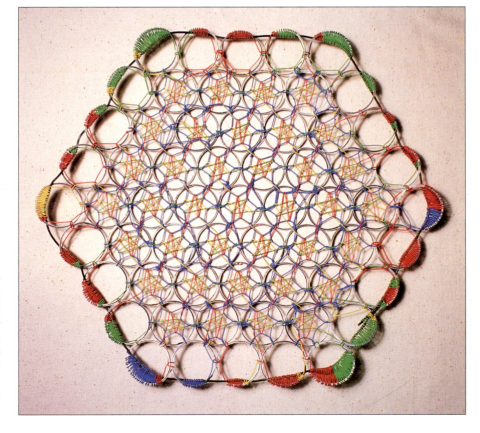

Drinks-can-rim platter
The metal rims are cut from the top of drinks cans and systematically laced together with telephone wire to make a hexagonal design. Another length of thicker wire is threaded round the edge and then woven on to the rings with more telephone wire.

Bottle-top bowl

This bowl uses a jar lid for the centre and wire is
threaded though bottle tops that are pierced through
their centres. The tops are carefully arranged to create
the star pattern. bottle tops are squeezed on to the
wires at the edges to conceal the ends.

Opposite
Orange-net bowl
This bowl is made using the nets in which oranges
and onions are often packaged. The nets are opened
out and layered over a beach ball. The whole surface
is then covered with a lace stitch. There are at least
three layers of netting worked over it. When
complete, the beach ball is removed!

Index

Plaited dish
This little dish is made from two pages of a glossy calendar, each one featuring the portrait of a girl. The two faces are set at right angles to each other.